EFFECTIVE
SURVIVAL STRATEGIES™

Defeating SCHOOL VIOLENCE

KATHY FURGANG

ROSEN
PUBLISHING®

New York

Published in 2016 by The Rosen Publishing Group, Inc.
29 East 21st Street, New York, NY 10010

First Edition

Library of Congress Cataloging-in-Publication Data
Furgang, Kathy.
Defeating school violence / Kathy Furgang. — First edition.
    pages cm. — (Effective survival strategies)
Includes bibliographical references and index.
ISBN 978-1-4994-6149-7 (library bound)
1. School violence—Prevention—Juvenile literature. I. Title.
LB3013.3.F85 2016
371.7'82--dc23

                                                    2015021639

For many of the images in this book, the people photographed are models. The depictions do not imply actual situations or events.

Manufactured in China

Contents

Introduction

It seems that the nightly news is filled with example upon example of violence in schools all across North America. In October 2014, freshman Jaylen Fryberg opened fire on five people in his school cafeteria at Marysville-Pilchuck High School in Marysville, Washington. He then turned the gun on himself and died of a self-inflicted gunshot wound. One victim died at the scene, while three more later died of their wounds in the hospital.

School violence is not limited only to high schools. School shootings have occurred in schools where students as young as six years old have been affected. On December 14, 2012, the world stood in horror as news spread about a shooting at Sandy Hook Elementary School in Newtown, Connecticut. The twenty-year-old gunman, Adam Lanza, killed twenty children who were just six and seven years old, along with six adults, before turning the gun on himself. A total of twenty-eight people were killed.

Shootings or instances that end in death are not the only types of school violence. Bullying and fights in hallways, in school-yards, or on buses are also examples of violence that have made our schools unsafe. Gang violence in middle schools and high schools contributes to the problem. Some violence starts online. Electronic aggression in the form of cyberbullying and threats can make its way into schools, where the problem is escalated into face-to-face aggression and violence.

Community members grieve by a memorial for the victims of a high school shooting in Marysville, Washington, in October 2014. This is just one of the many tragic examples of school violence.

What drives people to violence against classmates and themselves? Are these senseless killings and attacks just part of the "new normal" in schools? Sadly, school violence is not a new phenomenon. Recorded instances of student-initiated school violence date back to the 1800s. The facts show that inner city schools may have more incidences of violence, but no school or town is immune to the problem. There can be violence and even death at schools in urban, suburban, and rural areas alike.

So what can people do to stop the violence? Are there ways to make schools a safe place for everyone? Some schools have implemented metal detectors to check that students have no weapons on them when they enter the school, but do such actions really make people less violent?

As we continue to look for answers to these questions, it is important to remember that even though school violence can lead to devastating consequences, it does not mean nothing can be done to help victims or prevent future occurrences. There are many resources and tools available to help both survivors and perpetrators of school violence move forward with their lives. Many victims of violence have gone on to assist others who have faced similar situations. There are also individuals working on tackling the issue at its roots in order to prevent school violence altogether. Although there are no easy answers, understanding the problem and why it occurs in the first place is an important step toward making schools safe for everyone.

CHAPTER 1

WHAT COUNTS AS SCHOOL VIOLENCE?

Violent events are considered "school violence" when they occur on school property, on the way to or from school, during school-sponsored events, or on the way to or from school-sponsored events and are perpetrated by students against other students or faculty. School violence can also occur electronically. According to the Centers for Disease Control and Prevention (CDC), although less than 1 percent of youth homicides occur on a school campus, approximately 749,200 students between the ages of twelve and eighteen were victims of nonfatal school violence in 2012 alone. In 2013, 6.9 percent of high school students reported being threatened or hurt with a weapon—guns, knives, or clubs—at school. Both males and females have been the victims of school violence as well as perpetrators.

While deaths from school violence are quite rare, the number of injuries is higher. Examples of physical injuries from knives, sexual assault, and nonfatal gunshot wounds include bruises, broken bones, head traumas, and cuts. Nonphysical injuries are another tragic consequence of violence. Exposure to school violence can result in an increase in alcohol and drug use or the onset of depression or other psychological problems. The deep roots of psychological damage that school violence can cause students is evidenced in the fact that students who have been bullied either in person or online are two to nine times more likely to consider suicide than students who have not experienced bullying.

Some groups are more vulnerable to bullying than others, including students with disabilities and LGBT students, but all students are at risk of becoming a victim of violence.

Police officers in Los Angeles, California, discuss with parents and community members the increasing problem of gang violence in their neighborhood. Gang violence can sometimes make its way onto school property.

School violence can take many forms. It might involve a weapon, or it might not. It might involve groups of students fighting other groups, a group—a gang or otherwise—attacking one student, one student attacking multiple students, or it may occur one-on-one. Even verbal exchanges and written messages can count as examples of aggression. Any instance in which a student experiences victimization as a result of unwanted physical contact or an exercise of power can count as an example of school violence.

Mass school shootings are some of the most extreme examples of school violence. These occurrences involve one or more students bringing firearms to school to attack fellow students, teachers, staff, and, in many cases, themselves. These tragic incidents have usually resulted in multiple casualties and often have long-lasting consequences on students, communities, and the nation as a whole. Although these incidents usually receive wide coverage, however, there are other types of school violence that are far more common on school campuses.

Bullying

Bullying—which affects nearly 30 percent of all middle school and high school students and approximately 20 percent of high school students, according to stopbullying.gov—is very commonly associated with school violence. Bullying can include verbal or sexual harassment, threats, peer pressure, or hurtful rumors against students. Physical bullying can involve punching, slapping, kicking, biting, and other physical contact, or it may involve weapons, including guns, knives, and clubs.

The Internet can end up playing a big part in school violence. Although less common than physical and social bullying,

Filming a fight with the intention of posting it on the web is one form of electronic aggression, but there are many ways bullying can manifest online.

electronic aggression, also known as cyberbullying, has led to some devastating consequences. Not only do students post negative messages about each other or engage in flaming, but sometimes social media is used to plan events such as flash mobs or fights in school. Electronic aggression has become an increasingly difficult problem among teens and preteens. One study cited by the CDC shows that students who are victimized online are also likely to be victimized offline. Electronic aggression is one factor that can be used to gauge how students are treating each other. However, it is difficult to monitor and does not always lead to threats and violent behavior at school.

MIDDLE SCHOOL VIOLENCE

People may expect most school violence to occur in high schools because of the age of the students involved. However, according to the Constitutional Rights Foundation, middle school students are more than twice as likely to be affected by school violence as high school students. In part, that's because students generally begin to become involved in gangs in middle school, especially in urban areas. At the same time, parents are starting to give these children more freedom, and they supervise them less. Many start using social media accounts at this age as well. The combination of these events may create the right conditions for group violence or school violence.

Middle school students who have recently been allowed to go online and communicate in social media settings may not be familiar with the online etiquette, or netiquette, needed to communicate. Bullying and ganging up on people online may start at this age. Unfortunately, many parents feel that they should be giving their children more privacy or room to explore friendships. Unmonitored children also become more of a target for gangs looking to recruit new members.

Gang Activity

Gang hostilities between students—which are especially common in urban areas—can result in verbal or physical confrontations on school property. Gang initiation rituals can also involve violence that may spread to schools. While most gang violence usually occurs away from school property, the CDC reports that in 2011,

18 percent of students between the ages of twelve and eighteen were at schools in which gangs were present.

Hazing

Certain cases of aggression that some people might dismiss as "joking around" can actually result in serious physical and/or emotional distress to others. Hazing, for example, is a practice—sometimes seen as "tradition"—in which a group such as a sports team or other club subjects its prospective or junior members to difficult tasks or actions that are often physically straining or humiliating. Hazing rituals often include verbal and physical aggression against younger or newer members of a group. Certain types of escalated violence, whatever the motivation, may be classified as assault, aggravated assault, battery, dating violence, sexual assault, or rape.

In the fall of 2014, seven members of a football team in Sayreville, New Jersey, were accused of hazing four members of the freshman team. The hazing allegedly involved physical and sexual assault against some of these younger members. The incident divided the town because students stood up to the abuse and reported the abuse to authorities, which resulted in the cancellation of the football season for the championship team. The seven members of the team, who became known as the Sayreville Seven, faced multiple charges that included aggravated sexual assault and aggravated criminal sexual contact. The incidents resulted in cyberbullying on social media among other students who took sides to defend their friends. Some students who supported the football players or denied their involvement in the actions spoke out so harshly against the freshman team that they potentially prevented some victims or witnesses from speaking out.

After the high-profile hazing incident in Sayreville, New Jersey, community members came together at an anti-bullying rally. Hazing can involve bullying, but it is typically done in the context of a group initiation.

The charges against the students can carry heavy penalties if they are convicted. The accused students will be tried in juvenile court. Teens who are convicted of sexual crimes—regardless of whether they are tried as adults or juveniles—must register as sex offenders for at least fifteen years. The severity of both the crime and punishments reflects the importance of taking hazing seriously instead of passing it off as "horseplay" or a "rite of passage."

Although not all hazing involves assault or physical violence, it can still result in physical or psychological harm and, in some cases, even death. A 2008 study by University of Maine researchers found that 47 percent of high school students reported being hazed in high school, showing that it is a widespread problem.

THE ADULT VS. JUVENILE COURT SYSTEM

When juveniles (individuals under the age of eighteen) commit crimes, including violent ones, they are usually tried in the juvenile justice system. The goal of having a separate system for juveniles is to treat and rehabilitate juveniles, in hopes of changing their behavior and outlook before they become adults. If found guilty of a crime by the juvenile court system, a young person might face being placed in a juvenile detention facility, or he or she might be placed in someone else's care. A probation system would require the child to check in with a probation officer to make sure he or she is leading a productive and crime-free life. When the juvenile turns eighteen, his or her record will likely be cleared. This is done in hopes that he or she will be able to lead a more productive life. In the most serious cases of crime, a teenager can be tried in the adult justice system, which could result in harsher punishments and a lifelong criminal record.

While the tradition of hazing is often associated with college students who try to get accepted into fraternities, sororities, or other groups, it is clear these group harassment rituals span all types of schools and social levels. In inner cities, these groups often take the form of gangs. In suburbs and rural areas, youths in organized groups may also display violent behavior outside classroom settings.

Teachers and School Violence

Students are not the only victims of school violence. Many teachers in the United States report being threatened with violence

This sign is posted outside of the classroom of a teacher who was killed by a student. Ending school violence means ending it against all victims, whether student, faculty, or staff.

each year. Some report being attacked by students. As students get older, they can outgrow their teachers. Some high school students might feel less intimidated by their teachers physically.

In 2014, a Massachusetts teen, Philip Chism, admitted to and was charged with raping his twenty-four-year-old math teacher and then killing her with a box cutter and hiding her body outside the school grounds. While this is perhaps one of the most serious and extreme examples of violence against teachers, there are many teachers who experience threats from students. In an anonymous 2011 online survey by the American Psychological Association (APA) of nearly three thousand teachers, 72.5 percent of them reported having been harassed at least once by a student in the past year. About 50 percent had experienced damage or theft of their personal property. And 80 percent of them reported at least one instance of victimization on the job in the past year. Of those victimizations, 94 percent were reported to have taken place by students. The APA calls violence against teachers "a silent national crisis."

The APA estimates that, nationally, about 7 percent of teachers in the United States are threatened with injury each year by students. It's not just a high school issue, either. Forty-five percent of the threats are by elementary school students. Nearly 79 percent of the threats are against female teachers. Each year, about 3 percent of teachers, or 127,500 of them, are physically attacked by students.

Many of the instances of threats and attacks were reported to have been a result of students feeling that rules were not fair or that they were being unfairly treated by their teachers.

CHAPTER 2

BUT WHY?

If you look at a random sampling of a dozen cases of school violence, you will likely find at least a dozen different reasons for what might have caused each event. Each situation is unique. But are there trends that we can point to that tell us why this troubling trend is occurring? The Constitutional Rights Foundation states that "school violence arises from a layering of causes and risk factors that include (but are not limited to) access to weapons, media violence, cyber abuse, the impact of school, community, and family environments, personal alienation, and more." This shows the great complexity of the issue. Let's explore some of these ideas more fully.

Is It Bullying?

One of the first examples of a modern school shooting that was covered extensively by the media took place on April 20, 1999, at Columbine High School, in Columbine, Colorado. Two students, Eric Harris and Dylan Klebold, placed two duffel bags of explosives in the school cafeteria. When the bombs failed to detonate, the pair went into the school on a killing spree. They used shotguns to kill twelve fellow students and one teacher. Their actions also wounded twenty-three others before they turned the guns on themselves, committing suicide.

The event was one of the deadliest school shootings in United States history, and the media was quick to find a reason for the senseless shootings. In addition to blaming video games and a modern culture of violent entertainment, many people argued that bullying was a factor. The killers were known to be part of a group of students called the Trenchcoat Mafia, who were considered social outcasts in their school and were often loners who were picked on by other students.

Eric Harris (*left*) and Dylan Klebold make their way through the cafeteria at Columbine High School during their deadly shooting spree in 1999. It was the first modern violent school act covered extensively by national media.

There are millions of students throughout North America and the rest of the world who might be considered social outcasts, or be the victims of bullying. But most of these students do not become violent killers. Regardless, it's worth a closer look at the effects of isolation or ostracism, known as relational aggression.

According to the National Association of School Psychologists, studies show that some of the most destructive bullying takes the form of relational aggression. Students who are ostracized may also later experience physical aggression directed toward them. A study released in 2014 by the German Federal Ministry of Education and Research analyzed the literature available on school shootings. It analyzed 126 attacks in thirteen countries: the United States, Canada, Germany, Finland, Brazil, Argentina, Australia, Bosnia, Greece, Hungary, the Netherlands, Sweden, and Thailand. The results showed that 88 percent of the perpetrators of school shootings had expressed feelings of social conflict, and 85 percent had expressed a feeling of being marginalized.

While many of these students felt marginalized by other students, 43 percent of the perpetrators claimed that they had conflicts with teachers and school representatives before they carried out their school shootings. Whether the relational aggression is caused by students or teachers, however, the results are the same. According to the National Association of School Psychologists, the feeling of being ostracized activates the same region of the brain that is associated with physical pain. School socialization depends largely on students' relationships with other students as well as with faculty and staff.

It is important to remember that bullying and ostracizing do not necessarily lead to school shootings. Other types of school violence, including hallway or schoolyard fights, can also be the result of revenge for feelings of alienation or even confusion

Some students who are bullied may channel their feelings of alienation or anger by attacking their bullies or by bullying other students.

about them. There are also cases in which bullying may not lead to any physical violence at all. Again, each case is different and may possibly be the result of several contributing factors.

Is It Video Games?

One of the biggest debates in the issue of school violence is whether video games and other violent media are to blame for any of the school shootings that have happened since the 1990s. Many video games may seem to glamorize violence or desensitize players to the damaging effects of violence. Some vehemently defend the games, stating that the number of people who play the games and lead peaceful lives far outweigh the small minority who carry out acts of violence and feel influenced by them.

Violent video games were mentioned as an influence in the Columbine shootings in 1999, as well as the Sandy Hook Elementary shootings in Newtown, Connecticut, in 2012. When police searched the home of Sandy Hook shooter Adam Lanza after the shootings and interviewed people who knew him, they discovered that he spent a lot of time playing violent video games. A game that simulated school shootings was even found in his home. But no connection could be proven, and his motivations remain unclear.

However, one school shooter who lived through the experience does attest to having been influenced by shooting games. In 1997, sixteen-year-old student Evan Ramsey gunned down his school principal and a fellow student and wounded two other students. Tried as an adult, Ramsey was sentenced to two hundred years in prison and will not be eligible for parole until he is seventy-five years old.

Ramsey gave an interview from jail in 2007 in which he admitted that video games had warped his sense of reality. "I did not understand that if I...pull out a gun and shoot you, there's a good chance you're not getting back up," he explained. "You shoot a guy in 'Doom' and he gets back up. You have to shoot the things in 'Doom' eight or nine times before it dies."

Comments such as the one made by Evan Ramsey may show that the mental state or grasp on reality that some teens may have may be more salient factors than the video games themselves. Some critics of video games claim that many children and teens may experience a similar blur between reality and fantasy. While video games may not cause psychological issues, the games may help to shed light on the problems already existing in some individuals. Although it can be said that many mass killers share an obsession with video games, it can also be said that the vast majority of people who play violent video games are not mass killers.

The debate continues, with some arguing that school violence has been occurring well before the invention of video games and others citing the increased frequency of school violence since video games have become popular.

Is It Access to Weapons?

The easy availability of guns is often cited as a reason for the increase in violent gun crimes at schools and elsewhere.

Another issue that some people have pointed to as a possible reason for the uptick in school violence is the easy access to weapons. Gun control has long been a debate that has divided political parties. Some feel that access to guns should be limited and closely monitored, while others point out that it is a constitutional right and should therefore not be subject to any restrictions. The National Rifle Association has weighed in on the issue, stating that guns could even help solve the problem of school violence if teachers could be trained and armed to deal with violent students. Opponents feel that weak gun laws and relaxed family practices storing guns make the weapons too accessible to young people.

Columbine shooters Eric Harris and Dylan Klebold had access to military-grade weapons. Automatic and semi-automatic weapons are especially deadly because they do not require the shooter to stop and reload frequently. This accounts for the high number of casualties in mass shootings.

Restricting access to guns, especially military-grade weapons, may help to cut down on the number of killed or injured. But would gun control stop all school violence? No. Bullying or hallway fights might involve knives or no weapons at all. Additionally, school violence occurs even in places that have extremely strict gun restrictions, such as many European countries. In April of 2015, a thirteen-year-old student went to his school in Barcelona, Spain, with a crossbow and machete, killing his teacher and wounding four others.

While laws may help to limit student access to guns and some other weapons, it would not entirely resolve the issue of school violence.

Is It a Difficult Home Life?

According to the National Institute of Justice, a child who is neglected or abused is 59 percent more likely to be arrested as a juvenile than a child who is not. Abused children are also 30 percent more likely to commit a violent crime. This data may help describe why some students tend to join gangs or associate themselves with other violent peer groups. They may be looking for a sense of belonging or normalcy that they are not receiving at home. They may also be more likely to want to take out their frustrations about their home life in a violent way outside of the home. That might result in bullying of other students, mistreatment of others, or fighting at school.

School shooters and other perpetrators of school violence may or may not have had difficult family lives. They may or may not have had access to weapons through their adult family members. Each case is different. However, considering the home lives of students is an important way to look for trends in the troubling statistics of school violence.

Studies have shown that children and teens who are abused or neglected at home are more likely to get involved in illegal or violent behavior. Abuse may also lead to psychological problems, which may result in violence.

Is It Lack of Psychological Help?

Another factor that can contribute to violent behavior in students is depression or other mental illnesses. Columbine shooter Dylan Klebold was known to be depressive, and numerous other school shooters had been treated for depression or other mental illness. According to the website bullyingstatistics.org, bullies and their victims are more likely to suffer from depression than students not involved in bullying.

Teens might become depressed for any number of reasons, including but not limited to: bullying, abuse, trauma, social pressure, academic stress, and numerous other issues. While most teens who experience depression do not become violent, there are some who act out through violent behavior if they do not get

THE AFTERMATH

Perpetrators of school violence are not the only ones who require psychological help and guidance. Those who witness school violence or are injured in fights or attacks may experience long-term psychological effects. Schools often set up special counseling centers to help students cope with the effects of violence at their school. A supportive environment after a crisis or sudden loss in the school community is essential if students are going to retain a healthy outlook. Even students who don't seem like they are having trouble dealing with an injury or experience they witnessed may develop issues weeks, months, or even years later. Getting help for those problems is an important part of the healing process.

the help they need. Even small acts of violence and antisocial behavior among elementary school students provide evidence that students need more counseling and psychological attention than they are getting.

Even if depression and mental illness are linked to other factors, such as domestic problems, depressed or mentally ill teens exhibiting violent behavior need the help of a mental health professional. Whether a student is bullied by classmates and acts out in revenge, or if a student is mistreated at home and becomes a school bully, the issue remains that the person is not getting the help he or she needs to deal with difficult emotions and states of mind. It is important to note, however, that despite receiving help or treatment, many students have still committed violent acts—even school shootings—indicating that the problem of school violence is complex and must be tackled on several fronts.

CHAPTER 3

ADDRESSING THE PROBLEM

Schools around the world have realized the need to address the problem of school violence. Students spend almost as much time in schools as adults do working at their jobs. If students do not feel safe in their own schools, problems will develop within social groups, among school communities, and even among society as a whole. Parent groups, teacher groups, and school administrators have worked to address the problem in different ways. Even student groups have taken it upon themselves to help confront school violence and the issues that cause it.

Anti-Bullying Programs

Anti-bullying programs are being adopted by many public school districts. The programs offer teacher training and resources to address bullying and cyberbullying. They provide curriculums that can be taught to students on an elementary school, middle school, and high school level. Ideas such as respect, peaceful

Positive Classrooms is an anti-bullying program in Canada that has used different methods, including making an anti-bullying video and launching a kindness campaign, to help end bullying in schools.

problem solving, cooperation, and even suicide prevention are introduced.

A wide range of student violence can be addressed in school anti-bullying programs. From incidents on buses for elementary school students to dating violence and gang violence involving teens, the programs have the capacity to address the problems that schools are facing.

Character education is another way to improve student outlook through a curriculum. These programs are sometimes paired with anti-bullying programs. Educating students about the character traits that make up responsible and caring citizens can help curb violent behavior and help address the problem of violence. The programs target the six main areas of good character: trustworthiness, respect, responsibility, fairness, caring, and citizenship. Encouraging these traits and exploring them in depth could mean less violence and hatred among students.

Lockdowns

In order to address the unfortunate reality of living in a world where violence can happen in the normally safe school environment, many districts have adopted a policy of practicing for worst-case scenarios. Lockdown drills have become as common as fire drills, and they are designed to help students know how to react in the event that a violent situation does unfold at the school. The drills help students to prepare by teaching them where they should go if a school shooter or other dangerous intruder entered the school. Teachers and students both take part in the drills. Teachers practice telling students to stay away from windows and find safe places to hide, learn which doors should be locked, and how to keep students safe until police have cleared the scene for them.

The practices have helped students stay safe. For example, in December 2013, a student shot a classmate at a Denver school. Because of lockdown drills, teachers and students at the school knew to stay huddled in locked classrooms until the police evacuated them. Such drills have made students more aware of how to react and stay calm if danger does arise.

Limiting Electronic Devices

Cell phones and other electronic devices can be a distraction in the classroom, and many schools do not allow them to be used. But many schools also ban their use even when students are in the cafeteria or at recess—outside of the classroom when students are not being formally taught by a teacher. This is done to cut down on cyberbullying. Schools want to prevent students from texting to each other in an exclusionary way or to ostracize other students.

School administrations have an interest in understanding the feelings of their students and the challenges they go through. Rules that speak to such challenges can go a long way in helping students feel more comfortable or accepted at their schools.

School Counseling

A good school counseling program can help students deal with the problems they may be facing with peers or teachers. School counselors have the ability to spot problems and help students to deal with their troubles. They can be available to the extent that a student wants them to be, and the students' peers and friends do not even have to know that they are being counseled. A student who is bullied and wants to act out can talk about the problem instead. A student who is bullied and does not want to act out can talk over the problem and find a constructive way to deal with it.

But even the best counseling programs cannot work unless the students who need it are identified and take part in the programs. And that's the biggest challenge that school psychologists face. They may be successful with the students they reach, but the students who go undetected and unhelped are the ones who get worse and may turn to violence as a reaction to their problems.

Peer Mediation

Some teens and younger students may feel intimidated seeking help from adults, especially in a school setting. Peer mediation is an approach that allows students to help other students. Similar to programs in which students tutor other students in academics, peer mediation groups can be available so that students can talk about their stresses and problems together. Sometimes these groups may be overseen by an adult, but it's the students who share their experiences with each other and offer an ear to someone in need.

Help from peers can help students thrive in many ways. Not only can it help them to make decisions that could keep their

Talking to adults and other peers in an organized mediation session can have a great impact on the psychological well-being of students and prevent violence in the future.

schools safer, it can also be instrumental in keeping students from joining gangs or making other poor decisions about their future.

Peer mediation can also help students who have suffered the trauma of school shootings. Some who experience traumatic events like that—whether they are injured or not—can experience post-traumatic stress disorder (PTSD). This can have lifelong effects if someone does not get help. Some students who have gone through these tragedies reach out to other victims of school shootings to offer their support.

COLUMBINE SURVIVORS HELP

Survivors of the Columbine shooting have formed a support group called the Rebels Project and a nonprofit organization called Phoenix 999 to help the survivors of other traumatic violent events. The group offers online and in-person forums for those affected by mass violence. Heather Egeland, a cofounder of the group and survivor of the 1999 shooting, stated in an interview that, "We seek to encourage other survivors to believe that, while every traumatic experience is different, they are not alone in their struggles."

The group was formed about a year after a mass shooting in a movie theater in Colorado. While it was not a school shooting that inspired the founders, they knew the victims would have feelings similar to those they had when they experienced their own tragedy. Egeland stated, "The most important lesson we have learned is that none of us is alone. The healing process is long, tiring, and overwhelming at times. We all had to adjust to what we refer to as the new normal. The normal we knew before is not the normal we know now."

For example, student survivors of the 1999 Columbine shooting are now adults. But their memories of that fateful day at their school are still fresh in their minds. For many, the experience shaped who they have become, and they want to let other young people who have experienced school violence know that they are not alone. Some started support groups that offer help to other people who had experiences similar to theirs. This kind of help is perhaps the most effective of all. It not only makes victims realize that they are not alone, but it also helps them to see that they can one day lead productive and peaceful lives as adults.

Other Ways to Deal with Violence

Some ideas for dealing with school violence include putting metal detectors at school entrances. Preventing the entry of guns and knives into schools can help to reduce the impact of violent students. These metal detectors are most commonly used in inner city high schools where gang violence is a serious issue. However, they

Preventative measures, such as installing metal detectors in schools, can help schools create and sustain a safe environment for students.

have slowly become more common in suburban and even rural schools to help prevent tragedies from happening.

Other ideas are more controversial. Some school administrators propose having armed police in schools or even training teachers to carry guns. Some people argue that these solutions would be disruptive to the learning experience. Many teachers argue that their job is to teach students, not police them. They fear having to carry guns and feel it could increase the incidences of accidents or encourage students to try to obtain the weapons.

Although there are no simple answers to the problem of school violence, the existence of various programs to help prevent the onset of school violence or cope with the aftermath of it gives hope that the incidence of violent acts on school property will one day diminish or even end altogether, and that those who have been subject to such acts can go on to lead normal and healthy lives.

CHAPTER 4

WARNING SIGNS

After almost any act of school violence, people ask themselves what could have been done to stop it from happening. They wonder if they had missed warning signs, or what they should have done even if they had noticed a student exhibiting warning signs of potentially dangerous behavior.

In many cases, students do exhibit warning signs before carrying out acts of violence. But the existence of a warning sign is no guarantee that a violent act will take place. People who report warning signs often do so to be cautious. They may take the attitude that it's better to be safe than to be sorry when it comes to the safety of classmates and school faculty. On the other hand, reporting warning signs may not be enough to prevent an attack. Still, learning how to notice warning signs, knowing who to report them to, and keeping your own safety in mind in the process is an important defense against future attacks.

Talk to adults and counselors about bullying that is going on at school or any behavior you notice that might be cause for concern. An adult can help prevent a bad situation from escalating further.

Report Bullying

A bully is often easy to spot. Many times, the bully is well-known to a large number of students and faculty. If bullying victims fear that reporting the bully will either have no effect at all or that they would be putting themselves in danger, friends, family, witnesses, classmates, and others should consider reporting the effects that the victim is suffering.

Instead of naming the bully, focus on the victim and make school authorities aware of the signs that person may be exhibiting: fear, withdrawal, anger, or sadness, for example. While bullying is a warning sign of violence, so is victimization. Bullying is a problem in many schools, but revenge on classmates that stems from feeling isolated or victimized might make a bad situation worse.

Don't limit your reports to signs of student bullying, either. If you see a student being repeatedly picked on by a teacher or other faculty member, it's appropriate to say something to an authority. Anonymous reporting is also acceptable. It's the job of a school counselor or other authority to make sure students are not being mistreated or victimized in the school. That includes victimization by anyone. While some students may be afraid to get involved or to risk the consequences of someone finding out that they said something, they may help the entire school by preventing a potentially worse tragedy from occurring down the line.

Be a Friend

If you notice someone being bullied or mistreated in some way, reporting it is not your only option. You can also choose to make a difference in the life of those people who feel marginalized, excluded, or ostracized. Your actions can have a profound impact on someone who may just be looking for a friend. If a friend you have had for a long time is mistreated or

Sometimes just being there for someone can be enough to help him or her get through a difficult situation, such as bullying.

LOOK WITHIN

It helps not only to look for warning signs in friends and classmates, but to look for warning signs in yourself, too. Look to adults, friends, classmates, and support groups to find what you need and to get yourself help if you feel overwhelmed. Some people feel sadness or anxiety in social situations because they are being alienated by peers or abandoned by friends. The feelings may have a ripple effect, and students may feel that they need to retaliate against those who make them feel sad. If you do not have a trusted friend to turn to, think about the adults and school officials in your life and make an effort to get yourself the help you may need. The next chapter has many ideas for getting help and support.

bullied, stick by that person. Don't be concerned with your own image or reputation. Think about how it feels to be ostracized. If you know a friend feels that way, you would likely want to step in and make a difference, right? Some friends fear that if they are associated with a person being bullied, they are bound to be bullied as well. As a result, they distance themselves from the friend experiencing the suffering. This makes the friend feel even more ostracized and isolated, compounding his or her feelings. Being a friend—especially in times of need—can help to alleviate problems, such as violent behavior, that friend might develop as a result of being mistreated.

Notice Changes in Behavior

If you notice a friend or fellow student begin to act differently than his or her usual self, don't ignore it. Think about what is different and why that person's behavior might be changing. If that person is becoming more withdrawn, aggressive, confused, secretive, or otherwise odd in their behavior, consider whether you should let an authority know. If you feel uncomfortable telling a school authority, consider telling a parent. A parent might be able to make an anonymous statement on your behalf or give you the courage to address the matter.

Remember that there's no exact science to pinpointing warning signs, but it's often friends who can detect worrying changes in behavior. The APA describes different categories of warning signs, some related to historical or biological factors and others related to recent changes in behavior or activities. The presence of any of these behaviors alone or even in conjunction with

People can usually tell when a friend changes his or her behavior. Stay alert to any worrying changes, such as increased anger or aggression, that could be happening with your friends.

others does not necessarily mean a person will become violent. However, being aware of possible warning signs or changes in behavior can help friends be alert to future activity. The following are some examples of possible warning signs of violent behavior given by the APA:

- A history of violent or aggressive behavior
- Having a major mental illness
- Early childhood abuse or neglect
- Gang membership or strong desire to be in a gang
- Regularly feeling rejected or alone
- Feeling constantly disrespected
- Increased loss of temper
- Frequent physical fighting
- Increased use of alcohol or drugs
- Increased risk-taking behavior
- Declining school performance
- Acute episode of major mental illness
- Planning how to commit acts of violence
- Announcing threats or plans for hurting others
- Obtaining or carrying a weapon

Several mass shootings at schools have been thwarted thanks to friends and classmates who turned a potential shooter in to authorities. In 2013, a school resource officer at a high school in Trinidad, Colorado, received a tip from students that two boys were planning to carry out an attack on the school. Extra security was put in place at the school, and police were able to identify the students who made the violent threat. They were arrested on suspicion of making a credible threat against the school, life, and property.

In a similar situation, alert students at an Oklahoma high school told school authorities in 2015 about a sixteen-year-old classmate who they felt seemed suicidal. They indicated that the student was talking about and quoting other school shooters. When police were alerted, they searched the teen's home and found plans for explosives and some of the components to those bombs. The students' actions potentially helped to save many lives. Their actions also allowed authorities to get the teen help at a mental health facility.

In a 2014 case, a senior at a high school in Radnor, Pennsylvania, was reported to authorities after her notebook was found with detailed descriptions of her plans for being the first female mass murderer. She described her plans for killing one of her teachers and several classmates. The girl was arrested and charged with making threats of a terrorist nature. Her mental health issues are being considered in her treatment and sentencing.

The police superintendent of the town explained the importance of noticing and reporting warning signs. "There are always warning signs," he said at a press conference. "If you want to go back and reference the Columbine incident, there were numerous warning signs that went ignored, that went unnoticed and nobody took the proper action and made the report."

CHAPTER 5

GETTING SUPPORT

People who show warning signs of potential violence are not the only ones who would benefit from help. Victims of school violence often experience long-term psychological effects—sometimes even years later—from the stress and trauma caused by acts of school violence. Some never get over the event entirely. Post-traumatic stress disorder (PTSD) is just one of the many psychological effects that witnessing or experiencing a violent act can have on a person.

Lasting physical effects on the body are another possible outcome of school violence. For example, people who are injured in an act of school violence may be forced to live with that injury forever. Serious, permanent injuries such as a loss of a limb or loss of a sense such as eyesight or hearing can have profound effects on someone's life. One way to start reclaiming your life, no matter what your involvement in an act or potential act of school violence, is to admit that you need help. Helping a friend to seek the help he or she needs can also have a profound positive effect on that person's life.

Online Sources

A great place to start looking for help is on the Internet, where hotlines and online support groups can be found. Some are targeted directly at teens and have a particularly strong understanding of what teens face in their daily lives. Adult counselors and peer support can be found at sites such as teenlineonline .org, dailystrength.org, teencentral.net, and stopbullying.org. Students seeking help from online sources can do so anonymously, or they can do so with the help of a parent or other friend or trusted adult. Just because the help is online and

Some online sources provide support groups and counseling for teens facing problems at school and with friends. These are especially helpful for students who may not feel comfortable confiding in someone they know personally.

anonymous does not mean a person needs to go through the experience alone. The choice for anonymity is made available to those who prefer to seek help privately. The sources can also be helpful to those who don't have in-person counseling opportunities readily available. Most helplines are free, which makes them a viable option for young people. One source, teenlineonline.org, even provides texting and emailing options for teens who wish to talk about their problems with other teens.

Schools trying to start counseling programs can also look to online sources for help. The Centers for Disease Control and Prevention (CDC) has many resources available on its website for both preventing and recovering from school violence. The resources include indexes and assessments for schools that want to calculate the strengths and weaknesses in their health curriculums and their ability to deal with the stresses of school violence. It also links interested parties to initiatives for training youth groups, schools, and other community organizations in starting youth violence prevention programs. The site also includes resources for suicide prevention programs and anti-bullying programs.

The CDC is a good source for schools looking into assessment tools to help educators measure the risk and effects of bullying on all parties involved. The perpetrators, the victims, and the bystanders all have unique experiences and are affected in different ways. Schools should be able to address the needs of each of these parties when dealing with school violence at any level.

Counselors

A counselor, whether online or in person, can help a person sort out the issues he or she faces. A school does not need to have

School counselors are ready to help teens—whether they are potential perpetrators of violence or victims of violence—and specialize in dealing with the difficult issues that they face.

a specific help center, anti-bullying program, or trauma center in place for a student to seek help. But often, students do need to be the ones to reach out for the help they need. Even if you are unaware of your school's resources, reaching out to a school counselor, school psychiatrist, or even a teacher can help you get the care you are looking for.

Most schools have guidance counselors and school psychiatrists. But because their job is to help the entire student body, they need to be notified of a problem before they can help. Many school districts put crisis counselors on location at schools after a traumatic event such as a shooting or other violent action. That can be a great help to many people in the community, and it's a necessary part of the healing process for many people. After a deadly mass shooting, most school students require some counseling and guidance just to process what happened. They need the time to say goodbye to classmates and teachers who may have been lost. Counselors are in high demand after events such as these and need to stay available to students for as long as they need them.

However, everyday school violence and stresses of violence and bullying are often not addressed unless a student shows the need or desire to be helped. School counselors can help students cope with such events as well. These individuals are usually familiar with the school's operations and may have the means to directly address such cases of violence and possibly prevent future occurrences while understanding the emotional needs of the student.

Students who need help should not have to feel alone either. They can get help along with a friend who may have had a similar experience. Students who witnessed a traumatic event together can seek help together to deal with the aftermath of that event.

Therapists, psychiatrists, and other mental health professionals outside of the school setting can also provide help to students suffering from psychological and/or physical effects of school violence. These individuals may not be as familiar with the school environment but can provide an objective and safe space away from the school. Unlike school counselors, their services usually require insurance or additional payment.

Trusted Adults

Some students may prefer to reach out to someone they know personally and trust to discuss school violence. Teachers can be excellent role models for students, making a life-long impression on them. If students can reach out to these teachers about

THE POWER OF FRIENDSHIP

Never underestimate the power of friendship. Seeking help from friends can be a very useful tool for students of all ages. While help from friends is not considered "professional" help, talking to friends can sometimes give students the courage they need to seek help later. According to the National Center for PTSD, many victims of violence or witnesses of violence experience a sense or relief just from being able to talk about and tell their story and describe what happened to them. This is where a friend can help. The more an issue is discussed, the more "normal"—and less alone—the victim can feel about the experience.

school violence, they may feel like they are not alone in the battle. That may mean reporting other students exhibiting suspicious or dangerous behavior, or it may mean discussing feelings or fears after a violent event in the school. While teachers are not trained counselors, they are trained to deal with psychological issues that may arise among students, and they know where to turn to get students additional help.

Family members can also provide a safe haven for students seeking help regarding issues of school violence. A parent or other family member may provide an outlet for the student to talk to someone not associated with the issue or the school. This can be a way for the student to remove some of the stresses he or she is experiencing. The family member, like an outside counselor, is removed from the situation and can give an objective view of the situation and help the student find additional resources that he or she may need.

CHAPTER 6

MAKING A DIFFERENCE FOR OTHERS

The desire to help address the problem of school violence is strong among teachers and students alike. Students in both middle school and high school tend to feel helpless if they can't contribute to solving the problems that they face along with their peers. That's why peer mediation is such an empowering and helpful approach to tackling and recovering from school violence. Students have a lot of power, offering both counseling and support, and also serving as advocates for getting better programs into their schools. The first thing students need to do is show that they care. Then they can take action to show that they are willing to make a difference.

Peer Programs

Peer mediation programs teach students about conflict resolution—that is, solving a problem between two or more people peacefully. A trained student mediator facilitates discussion between the parties in conflict but allows them to work out their issues themselves in a peaceful setting. Peer groups provide an outlet for victims and perpetrators of school violence to find common ground and build healthier relationships with each other.

Joining existing peer programs in your school or community can help give you practice dealing with the problems that victims of school violence face. If no peer groups exist, students should feel empowered to change that and to set up programs

Teens can have a big influence over their community. These middle school students, who are part of the national group SAVE (Students Against Violence Everywhere), are protesting gang violence in their community.

themselves. Getting the help of a school counselor or other community leader is a good place to start. Peer advocacy groups are an important part of making a community aware of a problem. Just as the group Mothers Against Drunk Driving (MADD) formed from a grassroots effort in the 1980s and made a big difference in public awareness of underage drinking and driving, peer groups can make a difference in addressing school violence. A national student group called Students Against Violence Everywhere (SAVE) has worked for decades to make communities aware of the violence problem in schools by having students unite and stand up to face the problem together.

AN EXAMPLE TO SHOW THAT YOU CAN DO IT

In 1989, a North Carolina student named Alex Orange died while trying to break up a fight at a party. On Monday morning, his classmates decided that they did not want Alex or his good deeds to be forgotten. They formed the student-led group Students Against Violence Everywhere (SAVE). The group's vision is: "All students will be able to attend a school that is safe, secure, free of fear, and conducive to learning." Today its message is more poignant than ever. The group now has 2,200 chapters across the United States and over 220,000 student members. They organize workshops, do community service projects, and provide resources to students and teachers in the areas of crime prevention and conflict management. Students who share their vision and want to get involved can become leaders in their schools and communities.

Peer groups support not only those who have been victims of school violence, but also those who may seek help for feelings of anxiety, hopelessness, or anger in response to negative peer interactions that may lead to violence. Anonymous tips may also be left with peer groups, which could help to prevent violent acts from occurring in the first place. Peer programs even provide an outlet for students who may be disposed to violence or may have committed violence in the past. Many such individuals have gone on to speak publicly about what they have learned by changing their behaviors and encourage others to do the same.

Some of the many tools peer groups use to facilitate effective communication and conflict resolution include educating students on how to be both good speakers and good listeners. This may seem simple, but learning how to avoid offensive language and showing someone you really heard what they have said can go a long way to improving interactions between students.

Providing Other Resources

With the help of adults, students can set up groups that provide crisis counseling or hotlines for students in need. This can include setting up training for peer mediators or helping to choose certified counselors under the guidance and supervision of school or community officials.

Anonymous hotlines may be a way for students to inform others of questionable behavior and activity among their peers, such as a change in the way someone acts or a threat they may have heard another student give.

Students can do a lot to help prevent violence in their schools. It can be as small as helping someone to feel less ostracized or bullied, or giving a tip to school officials in the event of a threat. In

No one should have to fear going to school. With the cooperation of students, faculty, and community members, schools can provide a safe environment for everyone on school property.

addition, peer groups can do a lot to help students find alternate solutions to their problems and overcome past victimizations.

Students who can stand up for others can help show potential perpetrators that getting help is far more beneficial than criminal charges or jail time and may help to improve someone's life. They can also show victims that they do not have to be defined by their experiences and can go on to lead healthy productive lives. Understanding the role that average students and teens can play in the battle to stop school violence can be quite empowering. Providing tips, offering guidance and understanding, and helping to make resources available to everyone can make a school—and community—safer for everyone.

Glossary

ADVOCACY Active support for a cause.

ASSAULT A violent physical attack.

BYSTANDER A person who is present at an incident but does not take an active part in it.

CONFLICT MANAGEMENT The actions taken to deal with a serious argument, disagreement, or problem in a balanced way.

CONFLICT RESOLUTION The actions taken to intervene in a serious argument or problem and find a mutually agreeable solution.

CYBERBULLYING Harassing or bullying someone on the Internet, often through social media.

ELECTRONIC AGGRESSION Online attacks against a person's character, such as through social media.

FLAMING A hostile interaction between people communicating online, often involving profanity or other offensive messages.

GANG An organized group of people engaged in violence or criminal activity, often against other gangs.

HARASSMENT Unwelcome and hostile treatment of an individual or group of people in an aggressive or intimidating way.

HAZING The act of forcing someone to take part in strenuous or humiliating tasks, usually as initiation to a program, team, or club.

HOTLINE A phone line that a person can call for guidance, support, and help for a serious problem or issue.

INTIMIDATION The act of frightening someone to try to get them to do something they would not have otherwise done.

JUVENILE COURT A court of law specifically responsible for trying or supervising people under the age of eighteen.

NETIQUETTE Behavior that reflects the correct way to act on the Internet; online etiquette.

OSTRACIZE To exclude from a group, association, or society.

PEER MEDIATION Problem solving or conflict resolution in which the parties involved in conflict get help from people in their own age or social group.

PERPETRATOR A person who commits a harmful, violent, or illegal act.

POST-TRAUMATIC STRESS DISORDER (PTSD) A condition of continuing mental and emotional stress that occurs after experiencing a psychological shock or physical trauma.

RELATIONAL AGGRESSION Bullying that involves damaging someone's social status or social relationships, often through exclusion.

For More Information

Big Brothers Big Sisters of America
2202 N. Westshore Boulevard, Suite 455
Tampa, FL 33607
(813) 720-8778
Website: http://www.bbbsa.org
This organization pairs at-risk youths with community mem-
    bers in a mentoring relationship in order to help youth
    build brighter futures free of violence and drugs.

Canadian Safe Schools Network
229 Niagara Street
Toronto, ON M6J 2L5
Canada
(416) 977-1050
Website: http://www.canadiansafeschools.com
This nonprofit organization is aimed at reducing violence in
    Canadian schools by bringing together law enforcement,
    school boards, businesses, and other community members
    to develop safe school resources, perform research, and
    host conferences and other events.

National School Safety Center
141 Duesenberg Drive, Suite 7B
Westlake Village, CA 91362
(805) 373-9977
Website: http://www.schoolsafety.us
An advocacy group for safe, peaceful schools worldwide, the
    National School Safety Center offers leadership training,

school safety assessments, and student resources to prevent school violence.

Peer Mediation and Skills Training (PMAST)
1811 4 Street SW
Calgary, AB T2S 1W2
Canada
(403) 861-2517
Website: http://pmast.org
Through conflict management training workshops and other programs, PMAST trains individuals to understand the basis of conflict and seek peaceful solutions without resorting to bullying and violence.

StopBullying.gov
200 Independence Avenue, S.W.
Washington, DC 20201
Website: http://stopbullying.gov
This agency provides public information from government agencies on ways to respond to bullying, cyberbullying, and their effects on the public as well as prevention measures that can be taken.

Students Against Destructive Decisions (SADD)
255 Main Street
Marlborough, MA 01752
(877) SADD-INC
Website: http://www.sadd.org
SADD was originally started as an organization to prevent teen drinking and driving and has since expanded to include initiatives to prevent other destructive teen behavior, including violence, suicide, and drug use,

among others. Members provide peer-to-peer education and empower young people to stay healthy and safe.

Students Against Violence Everywhere (SAVE)
322 Chapanoke Road, #110
Raleigh, NC 27603
(866) 343-SAVE
Website: http://nationalsave.org
This student-led organization advocates for safety in schools. Members participate in activities and service projects focused on crime prevention and conflict management.

Substance Abuse and Mental Health Services Administration (SAMHSA)
1 Choke Cherry Road
Rockville, MD 20857
(800) 487-4889
Website: http://www.samhsa.gov
This agency works to advance behavioral health and offers grief counseling and programs to help individuals cope with PTSD.

Websites

Because of the changing nature of Internet links, Rosen Publishing has developed an online list of websites related to the subject of this book. This site is updated regularly. Please use this link to access this list:

http://www.rosenlinks.com/ESS/School

For Further Reading

Finley, Laura L. *School Violence: A Reference Handbook.*
　　Santa Barbara, CA: ABC-CLIO, 2014.

Hall, Megan Kelley, and Carrie Jones. *Dear Bully: Seventy*
　　Authors Tell Their Stories. New York, NY: HarperCollins,
　　2011.

Jacobs, Thomas A. *Teen Cyberbullying Investigated: Where*
　　Do Your Rights End and Consequences Begin?
　　Minneapolis, MN: Free Spirit Publishing, 2010.

Kass, Jeff. *Columbine: A True Crime Story.* Golden, CO:
　　Conundrum Press, 2014.

Klein, Jessie. *The Bullying Society: School Shootings and the*
　　Crisis of Bullying in America's Schools. New York, NY: New
　　York University Press, 2013.

Lohmann, Raychelle Cassada, and Julia Taylor. *The Anger*
　　Workbook for Teens: Activities to Help you Deal with
　　Anger and Frustration. Oakland, CA: Instant Help, 2009.

Merino, Noel. *Gun Violence.* Farmington Hills, MI:
　　Greenhaven Press, 2015.

Owings, Lisa. *The Newtown School Shooting.* Minneapolis,
　　MN: ABDO, 2014.

Smith, Marilyn E., Matthew Monteverde, and Henrietta M.
　　Lily. *School Violence and Conflict Resolution.* New York,
　　NY: Rosen Publishing Group, 2012.

Withers, Jennie, and Phyllis Hendrikson. *Hey, Back Off!: Tips*
　　for Stopping Teen Harassment. Far Hills, NJ: New Horizon
　　Press, 2011.

Bibliography

ABC 7 News. "Boy Armed with Crossbow and Machete Kills Teacher, Wounds Four Others at Barcelona School." ABC, April 20, 2015. Retrieved April 29, 2015 (http://abc7news.com/news/teen-with-crossbow-goes-on-terrifying-school-attack-in-spain/672487/).

American Psychological Association. "Helping Your Children Manage Distress in the Aftermath of a Shooting." Retrieved March 21, 2015 (http://www.apa.org/helpcenter/aftermath.aspx).

American Psychological Association. "Preventing Violence Against Teachers." November 2013. Retrieved April 16, 2015 (http://www.apa.org/monitor/2013/11/ce-corner.aspx).

American Psychological Association. "A Silent National Crisis: Violence Against Teachers." Retrieved April 16, 2015 (http://www.apa.org/ed/schools/cpse/activities/violence-against.aspx).

Associated Press. "Colorado School Shooting Plot by Two Teenage Students Thwarted: Cops." *New York Daily News*, December 20, 2013. Retrieved May 1, 2015 (http://www.nydailynews.com/news/national/colorado-school-shooting-plot-students-thwarted-cops-article-1.1554586).

CBS Staff. "Rage: A Look at a Teen Killer: Alaskan Shooter Suffered From Depression, Anger." *60 Minutes*, August 17, 1999. Retrieved April 29, 2015 (http://www.cbsnews.com/news/rage-a-look-at-a-teen-killer/).

Centers for Disease Control and Prevention. "About School Violence." Retrieved March 21, 2015 (http://www.cdc.gov/violenceprevention/youthviolence/schoolviolence/).

Chang, David. "Teen Girl Accused of Plotting Columbine-Style Attack at Radnor High." NBC, November 5, 2014. Retrieved May 1, 2015 (http://www.nbcphiladelphia.com/news/local/Teen-Girl-Accused-of-Plotting-Columbine-Style-Attack-at-Radnor-High-281378981.html).

CNN Library. "U.S. School Violence Fast Facts." Retrieved March 21, 2015 (http://www.cnn.com/2013/09/19us/u-s-school-violence-fast-facts/).

Connolly, Amy R. "Oklahoma Teens Thwart Classmate's 'Mass Casualty' Bomb Plans." United Press International, March 14, 2015. Retrieved May 1, 2015 (http://www.upi.com/Top_News/US/2015/03/14/Oklahoma-teens-thwart-classmates-mass-casualty-bomb-plans/1471426351670/).

Frontline. "Juvenile vs. Adult Justice." PBS. Retrieved April 16, 2015 (http://www.pbs.org/wgbh/pages/frontline/shows/juvenile/stats/juvvsadult.html).

History.com. "Columbine High School Shootings." Retrieved April 16, 2015 (http://www.history.com/topics/columbine-high-school-shootings).

Inquisitr. "School Shooting Study Blames Student Teacher Conflict More Than Bullying." August 31, 2014. Retrieved April 29, 2015 (http://www.inquisitr.com/1443422/school-shooting-study-blames-student-teacher-conflict-more-than-bullying/).

Jaccarino, Mike. "'Training Simulation:' Mass Killers Often Share Obsession with Violent Video Games." Fox News, September 12, 2013. Retrieved April 29, 2015 (http://

www.foxnews.com/tech/2013/09/12/training-simulation
-mass-killers-often-share-obsession-with-violent-video
-games/).

Konnikova, Maria. "Is There a Link Between Mental Health and
Gun Violence?" *New Yorker*, November 19, 2014. Retrieved
March 21, 2015 (http://www.newyorker.com/science/maria-
konnikova/almost-link-mental-health-gun-violence).

Mann, Denise. "Columbine Supports Other Shooting Victims."
Everyday Health. Retrieved May 1, 2015 (http://www.every-
dayhealth.com/emotional-health/columbine-supports-other
-shooting-victims-5913.aspx).

Neuman, Scott. "Violence In Schools: How Big A Problem Is It?"
NPR, March 16, 2012. Retrieved March 21, 2015 (http://www.
npr.org/2012/03/16/148758783/violence-in-schools-how-big-a
-problem-is-it).

Nolo. "Juvenile Court Sentencing Options: Typical Punishment
and Penalties for Juvenile Delinquents and Youth
Offenders." Retrieved April 16, 2015 (http://www.nolo.com/
legal-encyclopedia/juvenile-court-sentencing-options-32225.
html).

Office of Justice Programs. "Impact of Child Abuse and
Maltreatment on Delinquency, Arrest and Victimization."
National Institute of Justice. Retrieved May 1, 2015 (http://
www.nij.gov/topics/crime/child-abuse/pages/impact-on-
arrest-victimization.aspx).

Sanchez, Ray. "Massachusetts Teen Admitted Killing Popular
Teacher, Affidavit Says." CNN, January 28, 2014. Retrieved
April 16, 2015 (http://www.cnn.com/2014/01/28/justice/
massachusetts-chism-admitted-killing/).

Students Against Violence Everywhere. "History." Retrieved
May 1, 2015 (http://nationalsave.org/who-we-are/history/).

TeensHealth. "Should You Worry About School Violence?" Retrieved March 21, 2015 (http://kidshealth.org/teen /school_jobs/bullying/school_violence.html#).

Zernike, Kate. "Players in Sayreville Football Hazing and Abuse Case Will Be Tried as Juveniles, Lawyers Say." *New York Times*, November 10, 2014. Retrieved April 16, 2015 (http:// www.nytimes.com/2014/11/11/nyregion/players-in-sayreville-football-hazing-case-will-to-be-tried-as-juveniles-lawyer-says.html?_r=0).

Index

About the Author

Kathy Furgang has written dozens of books for young readers, including books for teens about fostering positive family relationships, surviving the challenges of middle school, and helping the homeless through service learning. She graduated with a psychology degree from Fordham University and now lives in upstate New York with her husband and sons.

Photo Credits